Catchment Area

Catchment Area

JENA SCHMITT

Carolyn Marie Souaid, Editor

Signature
EDITIONS

Cover design by Doowah Design.
Cover image: *The January Blackout* (mixed media on glass, 40" x 20", 2009) by Silvana Bruni, used with the permission of the artist.
Photo of Jena Schmitt by Rhett Andrew.

This book was printed on Ancient Forest Friendly paper.
Printed and bound in Canada by Marquis Book Printing Inc.

We acknowledge the support of The Canada Council for the Arts and the Manitoba Arts Council for our publishing program.

Library and Archives Canada Cataloguing in Publication

Schmitt, Jena
Catchment area / Jena Schmitt.

Poems.
ISBN 978-1-897109-40-3

I. Title.

PS8637.C44917C38 2010 C811'.54 C2010-902181-9

Signature Editions
P.O. Box 206, RPO Corydon, Winnipeg, Manitoba, R3M 3S7
www.signature-editions.com

for Rhett and Jonathan

Contents

The Restoration

> *Imagine restoring the night intact like that.*
> —Elizabeth Bishop

Imagine it was taken
away and given back

with a different name: day

being night and night
day. Imagine

the weight of it, heavy

as a limestone tomb,
a gate that guards

the dreams of everyone

but you. Yours are
hidden in floorboards,

archways, locked rooms.

Who will find them,
wonder what has

become of the person

who left the words
Fragile—Do Not Break

upon the broken

landscape? Imagine
night fell

but the fall was too

great. So often
the heart stops, the body

tries to escape.

After a Letter by Jane Austen

Aren't we
all sojourners in a strange
land, fated by a place
both realized and yet-to-be,

familiar yet misplaced
like moments near
the edge of memory?
Stranger still,

the scene of our inevitable
falling, a cubist
painting filled with angles
and obelisks, a series

of fabled gardens
and unadorned balconies.
Who knows
what the sky really means?

Look closer: luminaries
in the alley, thin
women and children
with parrots in their hair,

turning blind, misshapen
eyes to those steadfast
days and long evenings.
All along

the doorless corridor,
shadows of our former selves
waiting for their chance
to leave.

In Transit

This light, caught
between late

afternoon and evening.

First a rendering,
shadow upon

reckless shadow,

then line crossing
line, furrow,

arc and curve.

Men and women
in a rush, a blur,

their faces

like caverns, no
end in sight

but sighted, reveled

in; their bodies
open, unanswered

questions: *Time,*

where did it
go—and when?

This light, an echo

in and of itself, *o,*
o, on-again,

off-again.

Quiescence

Pay close attention to rainstorms, a lover's sigh, a train passing. Their meanings can change without notice. A test: if you roll a glass across the floor, does it hit the wall on the other side? Now map the room—fan, bookshelf, mirror, lamp, plant, table. Ask yourself these questions:

1. Can you hear the neighbour washing dishes?
2. Does every room have a door?
3. Are there water stains on the ceiling?
4. Does the yard slope toward the street or alley?

While fault lines can remain undetected, they can shift the course of a river or the foundation of a house over time. Remember, earthquake predictions about Istanbul and Athens were of little help. You are missing something, a glass perhaps, or maybe it is too quiet. The way the light falls or the window shatters, these are all hazards.

For Once

For once our destination matters
less than the rush of autumn
and the trees' inadvertent fury.
Their forgiveness comes easy,
faster than the bullheaded granite
along the way, the bare
bones of homes and businesses
forever for sale, roads dried up
like riverbeds and the slow roll
of tumbleweeds picking up debris.
Every mile reveals the delicate,
brittle skeletons of towns
unfit for the study of anatomy.
The study of well-being.
The spaces in between are
desperate to be filled, open fields
languishing under the one-eyed
gaze of the sun and the long
line of absent-minded passersby.
What remains is heartbroken,
built to withstand a lifetime
of neglect, with its faded signs
and crumbling vertebrae.
But this is not the place to
go back and admit that any one
of us, our far-sightedness,
is to blame. That would be
a different kind of understanding.

In the Attic

Even the mind must clear
the clutter of its years, the attic
filled with conversations,
addresses, people's names.

These are determined
as wasps to come and go,
and go again. Letters and photos
scattered like fallen

leaves, oh, how it rained,
the remains of silverware and bone-
white china picked clean
by a punctual yet untimely

bird of prey, age with its
rhinestone eyes and silly grin,
peaking around the corner
in a game of hide-and-seek.

The thrill of being caught,
but not knowing where exactly
and dreading when.
When the heart will stop—

Will it start again?
That insistent fortune-teller
with no fortune to tell, only
omens. Beware the mirror

that reflects no flaw or cloudy
imperfection. The memory
that ends as it begins,
locked in a small, windowless

room without a view to look
up to or sliver of light
under the door, its contents
growing old as those

who own them. Remember,
it was Tiffany blue, the sky
like a gift from above
and a tree swaying side to side.

The day was deeper than
that, almost black, a present stuck
in the tree, a cat, a presence.
No, not a present, a paper

nest and it was in the attic,
and the tree was not a tree
but a chair with buckling legs.
Even the wasps were

confused by their undoing,
enraged at the stubborn
but devoted armoire of a husband
who found everything

in search of a kinder day
than this, when not one hour
gave itself away, not one
keepsake, one secret.

A Fortnight of Drowning

When a river gets its way, the thought
alone is as real as any catastrophe.
It mimics the night sky and takes
the unsuspecting whose images reflect

meteorites and Perseid showers.
When frozen, everything goes along
with it, perhaps out of sentiment,
a way to avoid leaving, to be heedless

no matter what the cost. Because a change
in weather can fool even the most aware,
where green-winged teals are caught
on the water's surface, and at the same

time, free to go. But call it something
else, not patronage or devotion. Let's
dredge sediment that has settled
at the bottom, pull reeds and water

lilies out, pry rocks left over from ice
ages. Ask me about your chances
of drowning. Ask me how cold the water
is, how it takes your breath as its own.

Picasso's Women

Not intended for the faint of heart, myself
included. In the form of figures, decapitation
leaves one out of focus, another bending

over backwards, and yet another clearly
out of the picture. Peggy Guggenheim, perched
in her birdlike way, could've been a welcome

distraction, keeping everyone at arm's length
while captivated by art's men. That, too.
The mind's eye is here, in the stomach, or embedded

in the bowels instead of where it can be seen.
Consider foresight: time traveller
at times, patron at best, a blue-green

eye, depending on the colour of a shirt or storminess
of weather. It's the straight lines that need
contending with—a washed-out bridge, a frigate

spending its last days on the Sea of Cortés, Peggy taking
another look around: "Where are my damn sunglasses?"
Take away anemones, windswept apologies

on both sides of the rift, telephones or firecrackers
to communicate anyone's whereabouts.
Who knows the suddenness of indiscretion?

One said acrobat overshadowing one said dancer
or czarina. Light escapes them all, blames
its disappearance on the closest

victim. A sign: Lost pet. Fifi. Lost Picasso.
And while we're at it, let's chart this
distress in what could only be love's last favour.

This Evening

This evening
the half-light

follows the storm,
unyielding as

a child who
wants everything

and nothing,
throws itself

upon startled
ground to

see how long
it can last.

What little
consolation in

the words *there,*
there, yet we

cling to them
like boats tossed

about a violent
horizon, too

far to be found,
and too late.

Body of Presumptions

The draped, reclining figures
of Henry Moore
are heavy with possibility.

They never see
an end to the lines that weather
them. Eye after eye,

a hand inside a thigh
or around a pitted breast,
one of many

mounted and/or climbed.
It's been so long
since they've felt like this.

(Gasp, sigh) So long.
The delicate maquettes
will pay for what

they know. And then—
When this life is over
they'll simply start again.

Now's the time
to swim the pale waters
of the sky, revel in

the parts that are
missing: heart and mind
like phantom limbs.

They know how
to be the barest of bones,
bronze or stone.

After "Another Place" by Antony Gormley

The figures of men
are stranded

here, one hundred

of them along
the littered shore.

When the tide goes

out they rise from
the dead. When

the tide comes in

they drown again.
They are lifeless

yet full of life,

baptised, reborn.
You can almost see

them take a step,

look in a different
direction. You can

almost see them

catch their breath.
In certain light

they are ablaze,

bright as molten
lava. Soon they

become rusted,

charred, dark as
a shadow that does

not move. Seldom

do they stay
like this, willing

to be moved.

Perhaps one will
drift away; another

only longs to.

Catchment Area

An absence cannot be mapped. Like a word or name or street almost forgotten, it shifts over time. Take a collection of jade bracelets, an offering of almonds and figs, a letter, your poetry. They clutter a table or assume the place where someone else might rest. Nonetheless, you won't notice their intention: to show you what remains and what is missing.

The Flooding of the Elbe

The Old Masters can be kept from sight, but only for so long.
When the river swells, hands are quick
to judge as Raphael's or Rembrandt's: *Madonna with Child*

hanging from the rafters, statues at rest on every stair,
sketches as far as the eye can see, waiting
for the ebb of the Elbe. No room? Flood another gallery
so the jewels of Saxony catch the light of day. Like eyes,
they squint at the brightness, unprepared as always.

The drowned ones might be blamed for this
indiscretion, pessimists and defeatists who cry out,
"Catastrophe," forsaking Mother Nature for hemming winter
like a skirt. How short she wears it now. Against

prayer, against the odds, the water rises
to toast a couple's golden anniversary. To____, you old fool,
and to the lovely _____. You both deserve
all the happiness in the world. How long has it been?

Not since the symphony stopped
in its tracks and the Church of Our Lady fell to its knees.
Such is grief, carried along the swollen river, nearly

capsized, the subject of someone's art. Hold still.
A temporary Venice, no less, a chance to revisit
those gilded years when *Sleeping with Venus* had yet to dry.

Today I Saw Samuel Beckett

> *A voice comes to one in the dark.*
> *Imagine.*
> —S.B., *Company*

Today I saw Samuel Beckett
take the shape of a hawk,

steely-eyed and soaring

wide, eccentric circles
in the air. He comes to me

screaming, "Why did I,

did I?" and lands
on a lamp post, accusations

flying. I wonder how

close I can get, skilled as
he is in life and death.

Our sights are set: I am his.

The Stolen Poet

The statue of the poet
was dismembered,
a dead body

cut off at the legs
and sold for what
it was worth.

What it was
worth: two tons
of imposing bronze

metal. Only his
head has been found
amid the remains

of our modern-day
armour: worn-out
beds and unwanted

appliances, ancient
radiators, water meters,
temperamental

TVs and out-of-date
computers, discarded
cuttings, wire nests,

convoys of cars
and tractors sprawled
out like the bones

of dinosaurs. His body
floats in an endless
sea of debris,

not knowing
if he'll make it back
in time.

Back in time:
he stood against
an ageing skyline

and watched
the world diminish
in the dark.

After "The Couriers" by Sylvia Plath

"Love, love, my season,"
she ends and does
what she can

to believe it,
picks up the toy truck,
the broken dish,

the unfinished
manuscript. If the art
of repetition lies

in the convincing,
repeat after me: *a slip*
of fine, an empty

well. Like wheels
in mud they spin,
leaving spaces to get

caught in, first
a foot, then a limb.
Her words—

buried deeper than
any artifact
or ancient city,

a place few will
find when they
rise from the dead.

Landscape with the Sound of Wind

First the monarch was sighted, close to lifeless.
Then the wind. The wind was meant to stir something
within us. We were the guilty ones, overcome
and tarnished like tamarack. From a distance, the field
was wide open and full of the wind's musicians, leaves
like rattles and tambourines to chide and accompany
what was left. It lasted one, maybe two breaths. *One*,
two, three. *One*, two, three. Maybe three, this song
called hesitation. Soon the monarch joined in,
the wind giving her another life, a chance to live
again. Imagine: the monarch was dead, wings crushed,
neck broken, yet there she was, defiant in the face
of death. So this was how it was supposed to end.
The crowded tamaracks looking down on us, shaking
their weary heads. The monarch that never was
and the wind waiting for the rest of its fortune.

Figure of a Girl in Blue

It is difficult to see her, closing like certain
flowers in the evening, or curtains when
the light's not right. To see her, blue as
a flickering TV, blue because the air is cold
and so is she. Because she knows the moon
only follows so close, love-lost and soon-to-
be forgotten. Call her Persephone, maiden,
mistress, waiting for the long arms of night
to take her, sightless from this place.

S

To find the soul it is necessary to lose it.
—A.R. Luria

S recollects everything he's seen
and said, numbers and names and turns
of phrase that move image after
image in his head. Irises that grow
like spikes against a childhood
home; his mother in the window,
withdrawn and reflected. The shade
of Wednesday, blue-black like a bruise,
or an iris with its bearded bloom.
The weight of a word—*soul*—
like metal in the mouth, and lost
at the bottom of a lake. The time
it takes light to shatter like glass—

Apparitions

What we have
and have not

haunt us
like apparitions.

Should we forget
them, pictures

might fly
across the room,

lights flicker
off and on,

doors swing
unhinged. Worse

things have
happened, more

spirited forms
of redress:

broken glass,
images fading

into the wall,
phone calls

from the dead.
Like blue-

throated Shiva
in a tangle

of limbs,
what we have

and have not
are destined

never to part.
Together, they

can ruin
or restore us.

After “The Albatross” by Baudelaire

The modern-day albatross
has a different burden

to bear, a belly full
of lighters and Legos,

shotgun shells and marbles,
broken clothespins,

bottle caps and buttons.
Time goes by,

splitting the albatross
open, a piñata

with plastic bits strewn
like candy and confetti

along the sandy atoll,
all hollow bones

and narrow wings a mere
mention, a footnote

to its former self. Now
more mechanical toy

than sea bird, more
metaphor than Baudelaire.

Even he—the *poète*
maudit—had his

share of lost souls
and ominous warnings.

Inversion Theory

Equations predict chemical reactions and earthquakes, perhaps the beginning and end of desire. A handful of variables (earring, glove, button, key) solves any number of unknowns: a hiding spot or missing object, the distance between two people, two places. In poetry, the unknowable is also expressed by means of contrasts. And so oblique angles become straight lines, quiet becomes obtrusive, every house becomes a city. Even the words you write wait to be filled with meaning. If this is true, then you and I have changed places or have been misplaced altogether.

My Word

My word wrestles with its imminent loss,
forlorn as a mourning dove, the fatalistic
view an aerial and walnut tree alongside
the what-could-have-beens, the how-could-yous,

that hot little number called regret
and its unpredictable sidekick, jealousy.
They bask like cats in a patch of light,
stretched out, faces only a mother could love,

legs splayed, shameless really, heads tilted just
so. *Come hither, my feathered friend. Tu-whit*
tu-whoo. Let's talk about extinction, the possibility
my word will go the way of the dodo.

Can't say I didn't try, faithfully
keeping track of fainting spells, *ooohs, ohhhs,*
cataloguing dimwittedness, liver spots,
tooth extractions, maladies of the heart

that left my word excluded from every walk
in the park, every fête, every coo
and pirouette. *Mon petit chou,* welcome
to Witt's End, where edges are sharp,

so we walk on tiptoes, coveting ballet slippers
over salt and gold. Stupid idiot—I admit I said more
than once. Lazy, good-for-nothing. Yes, I was
indeed talking about myself; my word

long gone. Having had enough of these trills,
it became the most elusive, the most
deceptive of prey. Talk about revenge: eye
for an eye, wing for a wing, word for a word.

Blind River

Here we are, if not
in body, in mind, nearing

the river that cannot

see, that follows, then
leads, then stops—

The shore like a crowd

before us, the sharp
edge of its applause

giving in, giving up,

letting go. It leaves;
we leave, cutting across

sky and trees, ready

to drown or be
drowned, depending

on the angle of the hour,

acute as Lethe.
What is gone today:

yesterday abandoned

by the river that cannot
see, blind as the day

is new, is seen.

In Bed

The uninhibited page
attracts strange bedfellows,
commanding everyone
to look at me, open sesame.
Opposed to closed,
narrowing margins, the rift
between *to be* and *morning*,
asides coupling
and multiplying. The sheer
thrill, taking advantage
of possibility, a Brontë-esque
afternoon, a Proustian night
including pillow talk
and fight, sheets imprinted
with character, climax,
plot. For good measure,
a little foresight, knowing
what is to come and what
will be. All this despite
the slight, the assuming
nature of the beast, the many
sides of predictability:
Cerberus lifting a leg
to Hades' gates, Hydra
putting on a funny face.

Point of Vanishing

The mind corrects every image,
arranges our cubist vision to
try and make it right. Every view

becomes a map unfolding,
with a geography sensitive
to the slightest breath. One hesitation

and a building appears,
then disappears with the morning
light; an open field where

a house once stood or another
in its place. Turn away
and what remains: an empty

space the shape of an eye.
Memory roots itself
for a short time, discretely,

buried like a bulb in autumn:
iris, lily, gladiola.
With a change in perspective,

the map becomes a painting
in the same way meridians change
with every earthquake and hurricane.

Approach the speed of light
and time slows. It is closed off,
cornered, with no choice

but to stop. Each memory becomes
a beam in itself, edifying the present.
A roof collapses under the weight

of snow, heavy as Orpheus's
loss or a scar from hip to knee.
One does not move faster

than the other, yet the landscape
becomes dated as soon as the first
line is drawn. The street

begins to lose its vanishing point;
a creek buried underfoot; a bridge
demolished without second

thought; a quarry turned into
a park. If only this meant
the difference between February

and March, seasons misplaced
as often as umbrellas or gloves,
in lieu of more favourable weather.

If words lacked apertures, acute
angles would break the horizon
into pieces like a cup hitting a wall.

There might be forgetfulness.
Then regret.
Again the lilies did not take.

Forget the Muse

Forget the davenport of her
heart where you sleep
like a baby. The madrigal

that slips into dark corners,
under tables, between thighs,
ladylike hands redoing

the long face, the longing
in between. She, too, takes her
fill on the verge of another

fasting, this hunger a perfect
fit, a perfect voice for such
a song. Yet on occasion,

when you say, "Undress,"
her amusement overshadows
the reply: "Genius."

Figure No. 3

What is this love then,
but a reminder
of a particular August

night, a long wait
for something now
forgotten. Misplaced

like keys and earrings,
and found when no
one's looking. Perhaps

you'll come close
enough to say, "Don't
leave." But first, undress.

Four Warnings

> *What innumerable chains of fatal causes*
> *one's vanity, one's jealousy, one's*
> *cupidity, one's cowardice have laid*
> *upon the earth to be traps for others.*
> —Iris Murdoch, *The Sea, The Sea*

1. Vanity

More or less a matter of aesthetics,
where and when the tempest
will strike, a fateful bite

to match a wound, moored
like the moon in another time and place,
a lit-up *C* on a vast marquee.

Unfazed by the audience of one
in the same crêpe de Chine
and jewelry, a well-dressed

accomplice to mimic the affected
gestures and far-flung voice,
each overture louder, more

immediate than the last,
an unmistakable battle cry.
On cue, lights reveal a backdrop

of dead branches and tattered wings,
a mirror image that crashes
like a wave when it's through.

2. Jealousy

Every two-headed beast
must face what it does and does
not have, divided by an infinite

line that pits the body
against the mind, and so becomes
both predator and prey,

the reason behind its own demise.
Covetous of a distant past,
a small promontory from which

to see the view for what it is:
windswept, temperamental,
perhaps a bit impulsive, unwise.

Part of the recurring argument
that circles like a maelstrom,
furious, with no start, no finish,

no way to win but to take
the plunge, give in, wait for that
final breath, that lasting impression.

3. Cupidity

Pray the heart is an easier target,
now slower, fattened up,
stuffed, a trophy on the wall

of the unrequited, the damned.
One last chance to make amends
with youth's long-legged

beauties before their fettering,
backs reverent, bowed
like accolades, each craned

neck a pillar moved by regret.
Pilgrims attentive as birds
waiting to be fed, hand-raised,

trusting, with round, apologetic
eyes that reflect the water's
edge, the incessant giving and taking

away. And it does wear thin.
Many an enemy, love, can
cause such bloodshed in the end.

4. Cowardice

Where the trouble begins:
in corners unappreciated by day,
ignored by night, acres of land

unaccounted for, the sea taken
for granted, chastised, ruled out.
The perfect hiding place

to second-guess being found,
cowering, among life's
detritus, decisions left waiting,

tangled by the tide, restless.
Hesitant at every turn—farther
ahead, not far enough, too often

hushed by the trees above,
the middle ground between sympathy
and slight. A quiet warning

that disappears before the words
are heard, a lament that carries
on, in its absence, to longing.

Pinpoints

Wherever you go, you always leave something behind. At first, it won't be missed, not one note or letter. Please remember: objects and places might disappear into the air, but not without notice. To find your way now, a compass or map would be of little help. Like us, a city makes up its own mind about when and where to change directions. Without landmarks to guide you, try looking for fire escapes, street lamps, stained-glass windows, clotheslines, telephone poles. Where is the street? The park? Where are the red geraniums? These questions, though unexpected, are necessary. You see, like the night sky you will have to retrace your steps eventually.

Night Sky, Age 5

We telescoped across the sky. First
the Bears, then Andromeda,
Cepheus, Cassiopeia. "We might see
Orion," my father said. Looking
away, the collection of snail shells
on the window sill (my sister and I
called them sea shells, believing
Lake Superior an ocean) formed
the line of Orion's bow. That night,
she bit my arm until teeth marks
showed. My own constellation, small
and elliptic, the shape of an eye.

Astrolabe

> *Heloise my sister, once dear*
> *to me in the world, now*
> *dearest to me in Christ,*
> *logic has made me hated*
> *by the world.*
>
> —Peter Abelard

It doesn't matter if the letters
are untrue. Certainty can be
forged, landscape after
landscape, and slipped into
paintings or words as it often
does between lovers.
These correspondences reinvent
one another with every doubt
and longing. An astrolabe might be
remembered for its estimates,
for judging points between
the horizon and nearest star,
between salutations. A shadow
hesitates on the page like words
that are almost said.

After a Fragment by Sappho

Because I prayed
this word:
I want.

Because I held
it in
my hands,

an invisible bird
too terrified
to move.

Because I tried
to let
want go

and it came
back, demanding
more.

Because I knew
that voice,
paper-thin

and difficult
to place:
my own.

Sappho's Fortune

Beauty is beauty only while you gaze on it.

Love only love

when it looks you in the eye.

Look away, then

see what you might not otherwise.

Conversation with a Stranger

She worries
about comets and bombs,
poverty, recklessness, graffiti,

car crashes, global warming,
getting lost, losing limbs, never
laughing again.

She worries
the mind is a whirlwind
while the body stands still,

unwilling to continue. Conflict
of interest, tornadoes,
spontaneous combustion.

She worries
about being singled out, strangers,
particularly men, artists

who decorate fire hydrants
like cakes (icing, candied roses,
candles) and call it

art. What if a house bursts
into flames and no one knows
what to do?

She worries
someone will die, she might
die because of them. Freedom

of expression, food poisoning,
the end like a vulture
closing in.

Upstairs Room, Sky, Air

In a dream
the window is a door

that stands
between us. Asleep,

awake, nothing more
than the upstairs

room, sky, air
to keep us there,

in a dream.
The window is

a door, the upstairs
room is sky

and air, and nothing
more. The faint

lines of leaving
lead us there.

Empty Lot

In this newfound
vision there
is no church or age-
old oak, their
faint impression
in sunstruck glass
obscured by negative

space. The sky
dismantled, the heavens
brick by brick,
I-beam, relic, eyebrow
window, open
staircase. Emptied
slowly of all faith.

After a Line by Bei Dao

To be lost is a kind of leaving
that leads you to a vacant lot.

It leads you to the bones of old
buildings and limbless oaks

that stand like decrepit masts
against the vast expanse.

It leads you to the cattery,
the junkyard, mirror image

of the mind, land of neglect
and abandonment, of constant

longing and difficult goodbyes.
It leads you to the baby,

the stranger, the ghost, upturned
like statues in the grass.

It leads you to the sharp edge
of stillness, a wounded sky.

Portrait of the Heavy-Hearted in March

These days are greyer than grey,
lightless every time we turn our backs
away. Only the culprits remain:

the profile of a deadened sun against
the sky's endless list, its grand,
sweeping judgements. March is difficult

to take, impossible to change, like bad
news or the truth, and sometimes expects—
no—needs more of the same. One last

hail followed by snow and freezing rain.
And so the heavy-hearted cannot help
but make their way from Point B

back to Point A, umbrellas snapping
open like lilies or the promise thereof.
A meagre offering, gifts to the gods above.

The Golden Mosque

We are in a state
of falling,

like sunlight
against the gold-

domed sky.
Inside, the gilded

eyes gaze
upon us, ready

to strike and strike
and strike

until the walls
of fine white

china break
like cups

and plates. This
is the sound

divinity makes—
We hear it

long after the crash,
the crying.

Time Reversals

These are not solutions, only possibilities. And so you study snowfall and drifting tides, search through records spanning a hundred years for a sign, where once a century might be decades ago or any day now. Even cities take the shape of an ellipse, moving farther and farther away only to get closer together. You travel like this, right and left, forward and back, without a destination. At times, the landscape is elusive: a river mistaken for a corridor, a sandbar for a courtyard. There is a period of stillness before and after a disaster, sometimes not felt at all. In a case like this, close your eyes. Imagine it.

The Next Room

As with a dream interpreted by one sleeping,
The interpretation is only the next room of the dream.
—Howard Nemerov

Sometimes every dream is like this,
gutted like a fish
and left for dead.

For years my teeth
have been falling out. I cannot keep
them in. Not to mention

strange sounds in the kitchen
and giant insects
above my head.

The next room is a disaster:
ceiling crashing down
around me, floor caving in.

And when I try to scream
there is a dark hole where
my mouth should be.

A Misinterpretation of "The Hollow Men"

There was a time I tried to suggest
the Shadow as a metaphor
for death. Little did I know this
would be a longstanding debt:

death being death, and shadows
shadows. They are meant to
come and go, or fall like walls
around us when we least expect it.

Sentimentality

Sentimentality, my long-lost friend
who wants to be missed, who begs to
return, then begs to stay, who curses
Santorini for stealing the limelight
again. This is neither the time

nor the place to ask favours, our bitter
departure still fresh in my mind.
The day you left (how could you?) and I,
unsuspecting until the very last
goodbye, thought perhaps it was a joke.

In retrospect, the volcano was always
a threat, smoke and ash leaving me
in the dark, the caldera that could never
be trusted, its deep orifices, the thrill
of its sudden nakedness, the red

dress discarded, the centre of the earth yours
and yours alone. My competition
was steep and insatiable, desirable
qualities in a landmark, I've come to learn.

Afterwards, the ruins were too
much to bear. Sealed rooms, petrified
bodies, devastated pottery, neglected
frescoes waiting to be found.

Sentimentality, three times a charm
and it's been so long. Years of white
houses, months of basalt, days of
nightingales. Their cris de coeur speak
louder than words. Allow me

to translate. They are calling you,
of all things, jack-of-all-trades, snitch,
lady-in-waiting, understudy, clairvoyant,
and, last but not least, troublemaker.

Sentimentality, my heart indeed goes
out to you, the enemies made, the sympathetic
lovers weeping at your feet, not giving
you a moment's peace. And yet,
and yet, I've no choice but to let you go.

Lament at the End of Summer

By the end of summer the days begin
to escape us. Like thieves

they steal moment after moment

until it's too late, too many
are missing. Gone is the light, jewel-

like in the trees. Even the leaves

tremble at the thought of falling,
the dark clouds of starlings, the sun

more distant, more way-worn

than anyone. Days like these—
they give themselves away. And we,

faint of heart and weak-kneed, wait

for their confession: that the light
was taken, jewel-like from the trees.

How still it was, so close to willing.

The Poem is a Door that Suddenly Closes

The poem is a door that suddenly closes,
a clap of thunder in the middle
of the night. You wake, eyes wide, afraid
what is gone is gone for good—
a word, an image, a line. The threshold
of the mind like a fortress, complete
with corner towers and parapet, convinced
the door won't open again. After all
these years the walls have shifted,
a battle between them. For a moment
there is no sound, the clouds tethered to
the ground; what is outside has turned
itself in. The next flash of light: a branch,
a nerve ending. Now count to ten—

Hyperbola

Like memory, a city is not a place of certainty. Every angle and curve changes your desires: a building takes the place of another, street lamps and airplanes mistaken for constellations, circles for lines. You might blame this on forgetfulness, topography, weather, geometry or poetry. In any of these situations, distance can be as misleading as rainstorms or earthquakes, even leaves turning. Only there is more to lose than your way: the days in between. This is just the start, a premonition. If you look quickly now, the lake will be right behind you.

Fifteen Myths About Artemis

1. That time would forget her, leaving
   an empty space in the sky. A burnt-out neon sign.

2. She was once a man, or mistaken
   for one. It was the only way to get around now and then.

3. Her hair was cropped, her clothes were meant
   to hide the question marks
   her body made by being a woman again.

4. No one, not even she, could answer these questions.

5. The first "sir" she heard wound around her
   like a snake, a noose about the neck. Soon enough
   she longed for it, the loss of breath.

6. Her enemies made bets about whether she had
   testes or breasts. It was a joke among them, a contest:
   Who would see her naked first—and when?

7. Her portrait was commissioned by a man she
   neither knew nor wanted to. Let's
   call him X. It was never finished, the portrait.

8. She refused to undress or be anyone's mistress. In other
   words, she wasn't interested in sex.

9. Among other things, she was considered cold-hearted
   and ruthless. All those bows and arrows. She wouldn't
   leave the house without them.

10. She cursed her brother's name. O,
    how she hated him.

11. Orion led her on and not the other way around.
    Don't even mention Actaeon.

12. Her image can be found beside three-eyed
    birds and the many-headed Hydra.
    Fig. 220: Beast and/or deity.

13. She wasn't meant for this world.
    A terrible mistake, a disaster waiting
    to happen, an earthquake.

14. There were times when she was desired
    but not loved, loved but not desired. It was
    her greatest regret, how the two never met.

15. Someone once told her a myth
    is only a myth long after everyone is dead.
    She had no reason to believe it.

Why Hermes Left the Way He Did

Who could blame him?
He was sick of being overworked and underpaid,
a god of all trades:

merchants and shepherds, weights
and measures, fields and boundaries,
literature and thieves.

He was Io's hero,
Odysseus's saving grace (among legions
of others) and many a beast's recurring nightmare.

A precursor to Casanova known
for the size of his prick
and how well he used it. A patron

of poetry before poetry lost
its will, followed by prankster
and athlete, inventor and part-time model.

Don't forget messenger and dreamer:
when he spoke people stopped,
perked their ears and listened.

A tour guide to the Underworld,
he was matter-of-fact and efficient:
To your left is anguish; to your right, regret.

Anguish, regret. They were
with him when he fled—to São Paulo
or Berlin—and never seen again.

Variations of Home

A house can mean
many things, including
the formal *abode*

or *dwelling*. It can be a place
of rest, a stopover
between this world

and the next, or filled with ruins
and skeletons,
a veritable tornado of a mess.

It can welcome you
with open arms
like a long-lost relative, or turn

its heavy back, dismayed.
It can be shelter from
the rain, the wind that roars

like the sea, or nondescript
brown brick,
a methamphetamine factory.

It can be orderly, stark-
naked, white-walled,
what you call minimalist,

or the opposite:
dripping with this
and that. It can be a work

of art, a strange display or
a neighbour's eyesore,
every inch teeming with

wooden dowels and plastic
    insects. It can be gutted
and deboned like a carcass

to suit someone else's
    needs, be they modern,
pseudo-Victorian, Art

Nouveau or Deco,
    open or closed, light
or dark, the perfect

place to fuck and leave.
    It can be paper-thin—
hearing another tenant

urinate in one long stream—
    or built like a Cold War
bunker. It can look

like no one lives there,
    not a soul, or people
come and go as they please:

think the palace of Penelope.
    It can be abandoned
for fifty years, its contents

petrified like the bodies
    of Pompeii, or riddled
with *No Trespassing, Beware*

of Dog, Protect the Trees.
    It can be rambling,
raving mad, Grey Gardens

revisited, an ode
    to the Parthenon,
a monument to Greece—gods

on the roof, in every window,
        crowding the lawn—
or it can illustrate one

man's loneliness, another
        man's OCD.
It can be a sanctuary,

a haven for raccoons
        and pigeons, somewhere
to be heard but not

seen. It can be met
        with suspicion, standing
ovations, hisses, even

indifference, or it can be
        an abyss, a glimpse
into nothingness, a place

you'll never escape, never
        stray far from or want
to go back to, depending.

After a Short Story by Haruki Murakami

Each memory was now the shadow
of a shadow of a shadow

and every shadow the memory

of a memory of a memory.
They echo against the walls

around us or are sprawled upon

the ground at our feet.
Like a zoetrope, the wheel of life

circles, creating scenes

from circuses and carnivals,
a girl jumping rope, a galloping

horse, a ride in a hot-air

balloon. There are shadows
with long, tendrilled arms

that try to reach us, shadows

that make us feel ten
feet tall on a summer's day,

shadows that make us want

to run the other way. There
are shadows that look

like trains, strange faces,

volcanoes, the bars of a cage.
Shadows that remember what

we want to forget and forget

what we want to remember,
like light intercepted

with suggestions of what was,

the slightest *what is*
in this room full of ghosts.

The Numismatists

> *How much hope there has been*
> *in the past, all spent*
> *like forgotten currencies.*
> —Jesse Ball

How much hope there has been
is difficult to measure or admit.
When it comes to the past

we are numismatists who collect
recollections in the darkest
corners, drawers and closets.

Eventually, we know, they are
more costly if we never let them
go, and so we spend them

like forgotten currencies—old
hammered gold and copper
gods, emperors, eagles, ancient

kingdoms—until we are penniless,
our pockets empty. Has-been,
meaning time-worn, all but gone.

Archimedes' Prayer

His life is often thought of.
Not so much *how* he lived—
whether he had a wife or children—
but more for what he's done: diagrams
drawn, equations written.

When he saw the moon, the sun,
he saw area untouched,
the distance between them
a bridge, an invitation.
He saw parabolas in lieu of

doorways, pyramids amid
mountains, lines that pierce
like arrows everywhere
he looked. Images, explanations,
derivatives, the reason for—

the necessity of—*x*. He, too,
found himself lost in his own
abstractions. He, too, found
himself lost, his work
scraped clean and overwritten

with prayer. In murky-blue
X-rays they appear, translucent
as ghosts, a sea of floating
bodies. Just as he imagined them,
rising to the surface again.

Winter Storm

The snow turns
to sleet that turns to rain
that turns to snow

and suddenly that moment
snaps—power
lines, trees, telephone poles.

We arm ourselves
against the cold, the dark
with candles, food

and blankets until
the lights come back—
tomorrow, the day after that.

Not tomorrow nor the day
after that. Lights,
come back. With blankets,

food and candles we
are hardly armed
against the dark, the cold.

Telephone poles, trees,
power lines—suddenly
that moment snaps

and snow turns
to rain that turns to sleet
that turns to snow.

The Brontë Sisters at the National Portrait Gallery, London

Only one of the Brontës
is missing: the artist
who painted his image

in and tried to take it
out, hidden behind
a pillar like an apparition,

his phosphorescent self
beside three sombre-
looking sisters who saw

what he couldn't, that
life was a matter of time.
Like the scene

of a crime, the painting
holds—withholds—
reasons why: living

conditions, light or lack
thereof, the heavy air
around them, borrowed

books, drop of blood,
strand of hair. It may
have been sibling

rivalry that made him
stop and change his
mind, a rift that grew

increasingly wide,
knowing good news
would never see them

through their lifetime.
By 1855 everyone
in the painting had died,

and someone—either
grief-stricken, superstitious
or wise—folded it up

like a letter, unsigned,
to be found in another
century altogether.

Point of View

When something is lost, you might retrace your steps: shelf, autobiography, lover, city, winter. Or try to forget. It is a difficult choice. For every object you find (earring), another takes its place (button). Perhaps you look for ways to put the two together, remembering and forgetting. These are what angles are for, and long absences. Then it wouldn't matter where you went: Siena, Moscow, Paris or Osaka. If you were to ask me, you never left.

After an Unfinished Poem by Anna Akhmatova

And a garden—is not a garden, and a house—
not a house,
A meeting—not a meeting.
—Anna Akhmatova

At first it was difficult to believe
a garden wasn't a garden,
nor a house a house.

But then we were
on the side that turns
appearances into disappearances

as quickly as the night sky;
that changes loved ones
into ruins and ruins into

shrines, boarded-up buildings
with a thousand empty
eyes. They see nothing

but the consequence of time,
how it corners the present
in the past like an animal

or child, shows us how slight
we are as we slip from place
to place, afraid to move or be

moved. With every shadow
of a memory and sudden
thought we are taken over, overcome,

trembling like leaves when there are
no gardens or houses
or meetings to speak of.

The Land of Last Chances

In the land
of last chances

not everyone
sees the dead

ends and one-
way signs.

Some try
to make up

for lost time;
others distance

themselves from
what is lost:

days that feel
like hours

that feel like
days, all hands

and mouths
devouring them,

the weakest of
prey. So many

are heartless
here; so many

hardly mind.
They know

the end is
near, but not

the where of
it—or why.

The Loss of Loss

It's not age,
Nor time with its gold eyelid and blink,
Nor dissolution in all its mimicry
That lifts us and sorts us out.
—Charles Wright

It's the point in which we see the end,
half child, half thief,

settled behind the outstretched
arms of the horizon, ready

to catch a weary if predictable sun,
then moving on to the rest of us.

When fate gives in, it goes so far
as to find a place among the less

fortunate, collections of tired
and indifferent miracles left to fend

for themselves in a gallery of near-
forgotten hours and one-of-a-kind days.

Displayed like artifacts—one chipped
Etruscan vase, one death

mask, one unassuming piece of jade—
in an age where loss

is meant to be eclipsed by the very
best; two shadows that long

to be missed no matter how often
they try to avoid each other's gaze.

Next, we'll be told, turn the body away
from the soul, a necessary

gesture in return for a life well-lived
and lived all the same.

Heirs to an otherwise cluttered room
that knows no bounds but the sky.

Notes

"The Restoration": Quoted from an unfinished poem by Elizabeth Bishop (Elizabeth Bishop. *Edgar Allen Poe and the Juke-Box: Uncollected Poems, Drafts and Fragments.* Manchester: Carcanet Press, 2006).

"After a Letter by Jane Austen": In *Jane Austen* by Carol Shields, she mentions a letter written by Austen, where Austen felt like a "sojourner in a strange land" during temporary residences in Bath and Southampton (Carol Shields. *Jane Austen*. New York: Viking, 2001).

"After 'Another Place' by Antony Gormley": *Another Place* is a sculpture consisting of 100 cast-iron figures that face out to sea at Crosby Beach in Liverpool, England.

"Today I Saw Samuel Beckett": Quoted from the first page of his 1979 novella *Company* and into which I inserted line breaks (Samuel Beckett. *Nohow On: Company, Ill Seen Ill Said, Worstward Ho: Three Novels*. New York: Grove Press, 1995).

"After 'The Couriers' by Sylvia Plath": The first line is quoted from the last line in Sylvia Plath's poem "The Couriers" (Sylvia Plath. *Ariel*. London: Faber and Faber, 1972).

"S": Quoted from A.R. Luria, a psychologist who studied a man, S, whose memory capacity had no distinct limits. In other words, he remembered everything and forgot nothing.

"Four Warnings": Quoted from Iris Murdoch's novel *The Sea, the Sea* and into which I inserted line breaks (Iris Murdoch. *The Sea, the Sea*. New York: Penguin, 2001).

"Astrolable": Quoted from Peter Abelard's "Confession of Faith" in *The Letters of Abelard and Heloise* and into which I inserted line breaks.

"After a Fragment by Sappho": The first stanza quotes Anne Carson's translation (Anne Carson. *If Not, Winter: Fragments of Sappho*. New York: Knopf, 2002).

"Sappho's Fortune": The first line quotes Jim Powell's translation (Jim Powell. *Sappho: A Garland*. New York: Farrar, Straus and Giroux, 1993).

"After a Line by Bei Dao": The first line is a quote from the poem "Requiem" (Bei Dao. *Unlock*. New York: New Directions, 2000).

"The Next Room": Quoted from the poem "The Next Room" (Howard Nemerov. *The Collected Poems of Howard Nemerov*. Chicago: The University of Chicago Press, 1981).

"After a Short Story by Haruki Murakami": Quoted from the short story "Tony Takitani" in *Blind Willow, Sleeping Woman* and into which I inserted line breaks (Haruki Murakami. *Blind Willow, Sleeping Woman*. New York: Vintage International, 2007).

"The Numismatists": Quoted from Jesse Ball's novel *Samedi the Deafness* and into which I inserted line breaks (Jesse Ball. *Samedi the Deafness*. New York: Vintage, 2007).

"The Brontë Sisters": *The Brontë Sisters* is a portrait painted by Patrick Branwell Brontë in 1834. It can be seen at the National Portrait Gallery, London, England.

"After an Unfinished Poem by Anna Akhmatova": Quoted from the section "Poems, 1957-1966" (Judith Hemschemeyer, trans. *The Complete Poems of Anna Akhmatova*. Brookline: Zephyr Press, 2006).

"The Loss of Loss": Quoted from Charles Wright's poem "Two Stories" (Charles Wright. *The World of the Ten Thousand Things: Poems 1980-1990*. New York: The Noonday Press, 1994).

Acknowledgements

"Quiescence," "For Once," "In the Attic" and "The Loss of Loss" first appeared in *The Fiddlehead*.

"Picasso's Women" and "A Fortnight of Drowning" first appeared in *Prairie Fire*.

"Body of Presumptions," "After 'The Couriers' by Sylvia Plath," "The Brontë Sisters at the National Portrait Gallery, London," "The Restoration" and "Today I Saw Samuel Beckett" first appeared in *The Antigonish Review*.

"After 'Another Place' by Antony Gormley" and "After an Unfinished Poem by Anna Akhmatova" first appeared in *The Malahat Review*.

"Point of View" first appeared in *Grain*.

"Astrolabe" first appeared in *Pottersfield Portfolio*.

My thanks to the Ontario Arts Council, the Canada Council for the Arts and the Toronto Arts Council for financial support both in the early and late stages of the manuscript.

To the Banff Centre for the Arts, and to Don McKay, Mary Dalton and John Steffler for their editorial advice, which helped guide my work in its final stages.

To my editor, Carolyn Marie Souaid, and my publisher, Karen Haughian, for their careful edits and suggestions.

To my parents, Rainer and Suzanne Schmitt, and my sister, Sara Schmitt; and to Evan Jones, Gill Best and Silvana Bruni for their feedback and encouragement.

And always to Rhett Andrew, for his love and support.

Jena Schmitt is a freelance writer and editor. Her poetry has appeared in *The Fiddlehead, The Malahat Review, The Antigonish Review, Prairie Fire* and *Grain*. She lives in Sault Ste. Marie, Ontario, with her partner and their son. *Catchment Area* is her first book.

Eco-Audit

Printing this book using Rolland Enviro 100 Book instead of virgin fibres paper saved the following resources:

Trees	Solid Waste	Water	Air Emissions
2	45 kg	4,264 L	99 kg